W9-BGB-015

DEFINING CONVERSATIONS

DEFINING CONVERSATIONS

A Little Book About a Big Idea

Scott West

Mitch Anthony

Insights Press

Published by Insights Press, Rochester, Minnesota.

Permissions Department
Insights Press
P.O. Box 34
Rochester, MN 55903
(507) 282-2723

Printed in the United States of America

Insights Press books are available at special quantity discounts. For more information, please contact the publisher at (507) 282-2723 or orders@mitchanthony.com.

www.mitchanthony.com

Managing Editor: Debbie Anthony
Interior Design: Greg Wimmer
Cover Design: Greg Wimmer

ISBN: 0-9727523-7-4

Dedication

To my mum, for all the conversations that helped
shape my life, and my wife Laura—there's no one
I enjoy talking with more.
—Scott West

To Abe and Evelyn Lincoln, no longer with us,
the most amazing conversationalists I ever met,
and my brother Mark, who introduced me
to them and took up the baton.
—Mitch Anthony

Table of Contents

Preface

Recently a friend—who happens to be a business book junkie—remarked to us that he was embarrassed to say that of the last 12 books he purchased, he had only been able to read about four chapters in each (the first two and the last two) before putting them down.

What is the point of writing a book that is 250 pages if you only want to read a quarter or half of that? The question is germane to the purpose of the book you hold: *too much conversation today misses the point*. There's a whole lot of information being exchanged while the message remains hidden. The book you hold is small—not because it lacks substance—but because it lacks filler and fluff.

We have become impatient communicators, with a stopwatch instead of a clock. We feel a perpetual and driving need to jump to conclusions without navigating causes and effects. The technologies available to us are feeding our general inclination toward impatience.

Defining Conversations is a book about how to have conversations of substance. It's about understanding another person's point of view, paying attention to both their thoughts and feelings, and comprehending the significance of a conversation in the bigger picture known as your life.

We are challenging you to read this short book and after you are finished, incorporate the principles into your crucial conversations for the next 30 days. If you take our challenge, we think you will realize the potential we describe within these pages.

We want to get to the bottom line as much as the next person, but we don't want to miss the important thoughts and feelings that need to be communicated along the way. There are matters in life that are too important to be addressed by messaging. The true bottom line in life is that in order to make progress in business and personal relationships, defining conversations are essential.

Acknowledgements

Special thanks to the great Invesco VanKampen Consulting team—without you this book would not be possible.

CHAPTER
ONE

Are You Sending a Message or Having a Conversation?

We've heard it said that opposable thumbs are the unique feature that distinguishes us from the animal kingdom — somehow we suspect their highest use was not designed for texting.

— *Scott West and Mitch Anthony*

Recently Mitch's 12-year-old niece had a phone conversation with her grandmother. After she hung up, she turned to her mother and said, "That was weird . . . I said something and she listened; then she said something and I listened, and we just went back and forth like that."

Her mother responded with, "Dear, what you just did was to have a conversation."

"It was really different," was her reply.

1

To this young girl the back and forth of conversational exchange—the tuned-in listening and responding—was perceived as a foreign experience. This anecdote gives us reason to pause and question whether the world around us is evolving or devolving in communication. We must also question just how much we are being shaped and influenced by the communication forms we are using. Marshall McLuhan, the leading prophet of the electronic age, asserted that "the medium is the message." Our question is, "How deeply has the medium molded the messenger?" Are we becoming anatomical extensions of the technologies we employ to keep in touch? Are we beginning to behave just like our communication technologies?

Our discussion is centered on whether these modes of communication are helping us evolve into more effective communicators or hastening our devolvement into nothing more than messengers who send and contacts who receive—thereby unwittingly missing the vital linkage that substantiates communication.

Culturally and individually, we would do well to examine whether we are becoming more impatient in our communication with others. Are we becoming more self-centered—more clipped, bottom-line oriented, demanding, and dismissive? What role do devices and technologies play in shaping our communication behaviors and attitudes?

Ask yourself if the modern mediums for communicating are helping you become a more patient communicator, a more understanding listener, or a more thoughtful responder. One clear impact of technology on us is how it is eroding our ability to converse—often neutralizing our desire to engage in dialogue.

It is ironic to note that Thoreau lamented over this very topic of technological influence on communication behavior well over 100 years ago, with the advent of telegraph wires across the countryside. Because people had to pay for each word, he felt that they would necessarily reduce their communication to the bottom line. Words were literally measured with money—the communications technology era had begun.

Thoreau felt that the art of conversation and human connectivity were in peril and that people would soon fall into a pattern of directing messages at one another instead of exchanging the deeper chords of conversation. Sound familiar?

If you look at your latest phone bill, you may see a trend toward fewer minutes on phone conversations and a proliferation of text messages—paying by the word, if you will. For most of us, this is a good enough reason to opt for the unlimited texting option.

Today, however, we seem to have a slightly different economics issue—one that is more about the economy of time than money. We have become impatient communicators, with a stopwatch instead of a clock. We feel a perpetual and driving need to jump to a conclusion without navigating causes and effects. The technologies available to us are feeding our general inclination toward impatience and creating distance between real conversations.

Arguably, the invention that blazed the trail for the current trend in communication took place in 1935 when Willy Müller invented the first automatic answering machine. This answering machine was a three-foot-tall machine popular with Orthodox Jews who were forbidden to answer the phone on the Sabbath.

In 1971, PhoneMate introduced one of the first commercially viable answering machines, the Model 400. The unit weighed 10 pounds, could screen calls, and held up to 20 messages on a reel-to-reel tape. There was also an earphone that enabled private message retrieval.

The original intention of the invention was to ensure that people would not miss any calls. The unintended consequence was that people had their first opportunity to screen calls and avoid conversation. They could now respond on their own timetable. People were literally "off the hook" regarding the obligation to converse with a person or on a matter where they would rather not. If a caller knew the other party also had an answering machine—and had a good idea when they would be at work—the caller could choose to simply "leave a message."

The temptation to avoid face-to-face conversing when you could simply send a message had become real and actionable. Messaging had made its first major inroad into the space of conversation. Texting has now accelerated the messaging phenomenon into a dominant state of social intercourse. It is like a modern interstate highway system of communication where most of the traffic is flowing.

The trend in our society is toward *messaging* and away from conversing. But is messaging just another way to exchange information? Does it truly expand connectivity? Does it create empathy that binds us together? Does it propel progress? The answer is yes, and no. Messaging is wonderful for keeping in contact from a distance, giving updates, and for exchanging short and "quippish" ideas, thoughts, and whims. But we can only connect, empathize, and progress so far in the messaging mode until it begins to show its shortcomings.

Our modern communication technologies are designed for sending messages back and forth. This sometimes has the feel of conversation but is not truly conversing. Something important, something very human is missing in the exchange. We compromise connectivity when we choose messaging instead of face-to-face conversation. We are beginning to feel the effects of the downward spiral of connectivity and the natural temptation toward time preservation that these technologies create for us.

Have you avoided calls and face-to-face interactions, so that you could be in control of who you talked to and when? You may have felt insecure at times meeting with someone who needs to converse in person. Have you ever e-mailed someone in an adjacent workstation who is no more than 10 feet away rather than get up and have a verbal exchange? We are, in some ways, cocooning ourselves within messaging bubbles where we are in contact with people instantaneously but not necessarily *in touch* with them.

This trend echoes Thoreau's lament over how wired communication would lure us away from human conversation. We can't help but wonder what kind of conversationalists will emerge from the texting generation. If the medium is indeed the message, then the message is clearly, "Be brief, get to the point, respond immediately . . . and I'll respond when it's convenient for me."

So informed are we by our technologies today that much of what we call conversation is actually a myth—little more than another form of messaging. We are seduced into the deception that messaging is the same as conversing. We meet with people and tell them our thoughts, and then they tell us their thoughts. Far too often, the art of conversation is

Like texting and e-mailing, PowerPoint presentations often end up being nothing more than another form of verbal spillage.

lost in the exchange. Like texting and e-mailing, Power-Point presentations often end up being nothing more than another form of verbal spillage—an erupting well that can be hard to cap.

Don't get us wrong—we are not anti technology. In fact, we love the efficiencies technology offers. We both use messaging technologies each day and love having the expeditious and reductive option available when needed. But as much as the technology informs us as individuals, we also recognize how easy it is to lose touch with the borders between messaging and conversing.

Hopefully by now you agree that there is a distinct difference between sending a message and having a conversation. It's important that you stay in touch with those differences and use the available technologies to your advantage. One apparent skill is needed in your exchanges—being able to discern when and where *messaging* or *conversing* is the appropriate form of exchange.

Scott and I like to take our audiences through an exercise that illustrates this point in a memorable way. Participants are paired up and given a "communication kit" in which they find a mask and a blindfold. They are told that they are going to have a conversation about an important life issue. They will have the conversation in three segments of 90 seconds each. In the first segment, they are required to put on the mask and communicate via pen and a pad that they pass back and forth. In the second segment, they are instructed to take off the mask and put on the blindfold and resume their conversation verbally. In the final segment, they are unfettered from both props and encouraged to converse.

When witnessing the final segment of this exercise, it often seems as if shackles have been removed from the participants. The air is cleared of obvious frustration and communication impediments. They talk freely and in an animated fashion. At that moment we ask, "What does this remind you of?" Immediate responses include texting and phone calls and the shortcomings of each. We also hear the realization that people *tell* more than they *talk*. We hear a lot of "aha's."

We should all be concerned about the growing tendency toward succinct, bottom-line "groundstrokes" being punched back and forth without having time or opportunity to hear nuances of tone and cadence or the ability to view body language. When connectivity is at stake, there is no form of communication

When connectivity is at stake, there is no form of communication that is a suitable substitute for face-to-face conversation.

that is a suitable substitute for face-to-face conversation where one person listens and attempts to process what the other is saying.

When dialogue moves from a phone call to texting, we remove one additional sensory perception by removing our ears from the conversation. We can no longer hear the hesitance, the relief, or any of the other audible clues to emotion. We are trusting keyboard characters and symbols to interpret what the eyes and ears are designed to do—interpret emotion. This compromise is not without pitfalls, the chief of which is our brains being "wired" away from developing the instincts to converse about matters that require genuine conversation.

While the proliferation of messaging may really be about people wanting to get to the point, at times it is taken to extremes with many people outright refusing or circumspectly dancing away from conversation. In conversation, we can hear the inflection, feel the cadence, and sense the mood. With messaging it is far too easy to misread—we have "send" buttons but no buttons for "understand" or "interpret." A lack of practice in conversation makes for imperfection in communication. Ask yourself, "Have the messaging technologies influenced me toward being a more impatient communicator?" Our guess is that your answer will be yes.

Our brain synapses are being rewired into states of both avoidance and impatience. We are literally being wired away from achieving connectivity by the forms we are using to connect. In the next chapters, we will begin laying out the blueprint for how you can rewire yourself for higher connectivity through the most amazing medium of all—conversation.

CHAPTER TWO

Can't We Just Talk?

*Why assume that "great communicators" are always
doing the talking?*

— *Scott West and Mitch Anthony*

There is clearly a discernment issue about when and where to send a message or have a face-to-face conversation. The ability to make this judgment applies to all our exchanges, whether with another individual or a group of individuals. We are living at a time when we are in danger of losing the wisdom to know whether it is more effective to direct a message or to engage in conversation.

Scott was recently frustrated that his oldest son— preferring to text—would not make himself accessible for a conversation about a matter that Scott felt was important to discuss in person. When he asked his son why he insisted on texting his responses instead of talking, his son replied, "It lets me get to my bottom line."

This caused Scott to start wondering about two important questions:

1. **What is a person's bottom line?**
2. **How do you determine whose bottom line is more important?**

This type of rationale ("my bottom line") strips out concern for someone else's views and feelings. It is a telling example of how a technology simultaneously simplifies and complicates our lives. In the case of texting, it is a giant leap toward brevity but can be used to short-circuit connectivity and ignore the very heart of conversation, which is the investment of time and attention. Texting often gets used in a way that removes these essential elements of producing true conversation and reduces the exchange to the points each person wants to make. This is an example where technological progress has led to *less* connectivity.

———

Many of us simply don't know *how* to converse anymore. Conversation has become a forum for either controlling others or presenting to them. As a result, we often fail to comprehend the potential benefits that are only possible through conversation. It is this need to maintain control that subverts the potential for connectivity and understanding.

The myth of "safety through control" is sterilizing our conversations to the point of impotence, where we often mistakenly believe we can stay in control of the interaction and the result. Consequently, in our obsession to control, we try to map out the exchange—what points to make and when to respond. For example, if you are a skier, you may prefer the nicely groomed trails because you can see the terrain under your skis. Deep powder may make you apprehensive because you cannot see the terrain—you feel less in control.

Those of us who believe we must map out an exchange to stay in control often end up short-circuiting the connection. The need to control every step of every exchange is a flaw that cripples our exchanges. This may explain why in business and life we have become a society of presenters instead of conversers. Think of the business meetings that you may be forced to sit through while your colleagues plow through interminable presentations detailing their ideas and so-called insights.

You may come to the next meeting with your own presentation, somehow imagining that you will "PowerPoint" your way to mutual conclusions and progress.

PowerPoint has become the archetype for exchanges. Generating power behind "points" now masquerades as a group conversation, bearing little resemblance to a real conversation. "Go ahead and put together your deck of points, and I will respond with a deck of my own!" The gift of gab has migrated to the gift of jab as we spar with one another using messaging and presentation volleys. It has become another form of one-upmanship. There is a very good reason that these slides are filled with *bullet* points—they are aimed at somebody.

There is a very good reason that these slides are filled with bullet *points—they are aimed at somebody.*

How much meeting time and frustration could we save by tossing aside the slides and engaging in the art of conversation instead? Consider that there are many matters in life that are too important to be addressed by messaging technologies or PowerPoint presentations.

How many times have you walked into an important conversation only to walk away disappointed? How often in dialogue have you felt dismissed, trivialized, ignored, or coerced? How frequently have you left feeling insignificant and alone in your concerns?

One of the first problems that we see is a lack of *curiosity*. For example, have you ever walked away from an exchange truly offended by the other person's lack of inquisitiveness? The conventional wisdom is that if you don't get the other person talking within the first 20 seconds of conversation, the potential for connectivity has been lost or greatly compromised. And we all know what it feels like to be unplugged from a conversation!

Lacking the fundamental curiosity necessary for conversing, people often play games in the name of conversation. They try to manipulate and dominate others. They put up "counterfeits" that on the surface sound like conversation but that are, in fact, camouflaged forms of communication designed to gain the upper hand, all the while looking like a team player. This book is about changing that paradigm—exposing the counterfeits and defining the authentic exchange.

So, how exactly do we define conversation, and why would we write a book about something that on the surface seems so obvious? We have two compelling reasons to look under the surface of what often passes for conversation and get to the very soul of what conversation is meant to be:

1. **Humans have a core (innate) need to connect through conversation.**
2. **An incredible satisfaction occurs at the apex of a great conversation.**

Our goal with this little book is to deliver a big message. We want to stir a sense of longing for the satisfaction that can only be found in a real conversation. We do not want to let you (or ourselves) off the hook for accepting some cheapened form of exchange that may masquerade as conversation but in reality is so much less. As a culture, we have accepted poor, tawdry substitutes. It is as if we rejected the full-course, sit-down gourmet meal and opted for the drive-through menu. Have you ever had a really great conversation while picking up dinner at the drive-through? Neither have we.

Have you ever had a really great conversation while picking up dinner at the drive-through?

We do not deny that, as a culture, we are time impoverished. But the consequences have spilled over into our degree of connectivity with other humans. We have frayed connections—or none at all—because we don't take time for genuine conversation. Just as we don't sit down to eat and enjoy a full-course meal very often, we also don't make time for a full-course conversation.

This is a book about how to have conversations of substance. It is a book about understanding the other person's point of view (POV), hearing both thoughts and feelings on a topic, and comprehending the significance of a conversation in the bigger picture that is your life. This moment in conversation contains all the moments that have come before it. If the right things are heard and said, then the next conversation has the potential to become memorable and defining.

Once you master the point of conversation—either as an initiator or respondent—others will recognize it immediately, and your credibility will rise, as will the quality of people who seek you out.

What is the tipping point of the best conversations you've ever had? We are betting it was when the other party really wanted to know something—and you knew they wanted to know—for the right reasons. In other words, the point of the conversation was transparently clear, and it was agreeable to you.

In this book we will be introducing a powerful question that will act as a magnetic force and introduce a new power into your life. We have found that this question, like a homing instinct, will guide you wisely through every important exchange. Knowing you will ask this question at the end of an important dialogue will have a profound impact on the words and tone you choose and the manner in which you conduct yourself during the course of conversation.

Knowing you are planning to ask this question will sharpen your focus and force you to be accountable in conversations where you are approached by others with matters on their mind. It is a way of making yourself accountable in conversation. If your hope is, "I want to be trusted. I want to be respected. I want to help people feel that their time with me was worth their while," then you will want to begin introducing this question into your most important conversations.

In this book we will attempt to answer three questions:

1. **What is a conversation?**
2. **Is there a natural course to conversation?**
3. **How do we define an outstanding conversation?**

It is important to understand what does, and does not, constitute a conversation. Of equal importance is your ability to detect counterfeit conversations and the saboteurs that can derail your exchanges. Once you discover the natural course of conversation and the satisfaction and dignity it brings, you will no longer be satisfied with cheap substitutes. You will seek out conversation for the satisfaction it brings.

There are some issues that just happen to be the most important matters in life and business—the ones best discovered and resolved in conversation. If you gain the necessary confidence in your skills as a conversationalist, you will not give into the lures of presenting, telling, and controlling.

Instead, as you develop in the art of conversing, you will truly engage others, achieve mutuality, and achieve the connectivity that breeds success in every realm of life. Great conversationalists recognize that results don't happen just because messages are sent, but because we connect with others through *defining conversations.*

Can we get you to lay aside that electronic leash for a moment? Can we ask that you close the laptop and bury your deck of slides? Can we just talk? We mean really talk . . . so we all walk away knowing something important was exchanged.

CHAPTER THREE

Conversational Opportunity Knocking

To be effective, conversation must be I/you not I/it.

— Anonymous

You usually know when you are headed into an important exchange—a big conversation—where you have something significant to gain or lose. It's that conversation where what you could lose would be difficult to recover, and when what you could gain may never appear again. In other words, you have one opportunity to make it work.

While you may know when you are steering into a conversation worth considering, you may not always recognize the level of importance when that conversation is headed toward you. While the incoming conversation may not necessarily be a significant matter to you, it may be of weighty concern and considerable importance to the person approaching you—that person has an emotional investment in it. This is the place where great danger lurks—where you can unwittingly sabotage the individual's trust by underestimating the significance of the approaching dialogue.

What are the most common reasons that people come together to converse? Following is a short list that we have categorized according to the potential degree of emotion invested in the exchange:

Minimal Emotional Investment
- **Casual discussion**
- **Information exchange**
- **Brainstorming**

Significant Emotional Investment
- **Persuasion**
- **Negotiation**
- **Problem solving**
- **Conflict resolution**
- **Disagreement**
- **Apology**

- **Sharing of experience**
- **Sharing of concern**

When we are in chit-chat mode or simply exchanging information, there is little threat and less need for vigilance toward visceral elements. The exchange is, for the most part, not emotionally charged. In this form of conversational exchange, the only real dangers that exist are in being less than truthful or slipping into insult, disregard, austerity, or condescension. We must simply show respect to others as they speak.

In brainstorming we operate in a context of playing or exploring. It is one of the rare forms of conversation where people are fairly comfortable with chaos and disorder (therefore the "storm" part of brainstorming) before entering any form of order.

We would do well to expand our comfort zone with chaos, especially as it concerns the *significant investment* arenas of conversation highlighted above. The significant investment of emotions we bring when we are persuading, negotiating, disagreeing, problem solving, or apologizing more often than not causes us to be prematurely intent on achieving order and pushing for resolution—to the extent that the premature push for order short-circuits the result we hope to achieve. Our need to control in conversations paradoxically leads to an actual lack and loss of control in the situation. By pushing too hard and fast in conversation, our need for control backfires on us.

By pushing too hard and fast in conversation, our need for control backfires on us.

A skill worth developing in significant conversations is the ability to *call the audible*. Peyton Manning, one of the greatest quarterbacks to ever play the game of football, is a master of giving the impression of chaos as he surveys the defense and barks out spontaneous orders to his teammates. In fact, it is his willingness and flexibility toward abandoning the preset agenda and going toward the openings that make him stand out in these situations. This state of mind—embracing and reading the defense and calling the audible—can serve us so much better than the written-in-granite conversational game plan that is unleashed at "hello."

When *persuading*, we are looking to move someone toward our position. *Negotiations* can be either tug-of-war or a merging of paths, depending on the spirit we bring to the conversation. *Problem solving* is really another form of negotiation. *Disagreements* are like the flipside of brainstorming—where the same process of playing or exploring solutions would bring a more mutual air to the conversation. Often, we have too much emotion invested in our particular point of view. In *apologies*, we are fragile, hoping for forgiveness and harmony, and typically desiring to end the conversation as soon as possible.

All of the above are examples of conversations where the emotional investment is significant enough to require vigilance from both sides. Success in these situations requires a flexible frame of mind to *call the audible*—to go with whatever openings appear—instead of getting locked into prescripted agendas. You know well the feeling of conversing with individuals who have prescripted agendas. No matter what you say or how you say it, they drone on as if their position is carved in stone. In this case, think of the gray matter of the brain as cement, thoroughly mixed and well-set.

Remember the frustration of trying to arrive at a compromise with individuals who are obsessed with an *item* on their mental agenda? These individuals want it done their way or not at all. They want to cross off each point on their to-do list, no matter who is pushed or coerced in the process.

But, you might object, isn't one of the reasons for having a conversation to discuss a *matter?*

True enough, but don't ever forget that the matter is being bantered about by a *person*—someone whose dignity often hangs in the balance during the course of the conversation. When the matter becomes more important than the person, you have lost sight of the greatest achievable objective in conversation—*connectivity*. Your objectives are all the more attainable when you are connected to the people who can help you.

This oversight—the lack of weighing result and relationship—is the great blind spot of the "I/it" conversationalists who, swerving about with their opinions, insistence, and persistence about *it*, sideswipe the emotions and egos of others and build their own gallery of detractors. The conversation may indeed be about a matter, but it will soon evolve into a hunt once the other person senses a lack of respect.

If relationships matter to you, and if you want to ensure results, then every conversation must be about

"I/you." We are all branded by what we bring to—and take from—conversations. This aspect of our character contributes to our legacy as human beings. "What a wonderful lady she is," you hear someone saying about the woman who, with genuine curiosity, seeks to learn as much as possible about other people and their ideas. "I'm absolutely exhausted," someone else will say after conversing with her polar opposite—the rambling, opining, spouting volcano of self-indulgence. Great conversationalists recognize this fundamental truth: *The biggest opportunity in conversation is the possibility of connecting with another human being in a meaningful way.*

The biggest opportunity in conversation is the possibility of connecting with another human being in a meaningful way.

What is at stake in conversation? Is it an exaggeration to say that our progress, potential, and relationships are all at stake when we uphold our end of the conversational bargain? How can we fail in conversations and expect to succeed in life?

Consider that your relationships rise and fall based on the quality of your exchanges. It doesn't take more than two or three disappointing conversations for you to give up on the prospect of connecting with a particular person. Once you sense that the other person's vision is restricted to the tip of the nose inward, it will not take long for you to write him or her off as *not worth your time.*

When we are forced to converse with self-interested individuals through business or family, we learn to resent them and, at best, to feign interest in the exchange. While no one wants to be thought of as a person that others resent and endure, by failing to master the art of conversation, that is exactly what we risk becoming in life. Avoiding this fate is really a matter of paying more attention to people than to your own agenda.

Conversations set people apart—either in isolation or in veneration. It is in the exchange of conversation that we connect or disconnect with people, promote or impede progress, affirm or deny our credibility, and seal our legacy and reputation.

By recognizing the potential power of your conversations, you can begin to place emphasis where it has the most impact in your life—on connecting significantly with another human being. Such connectivity is only possible through one type of interaction: *the conversation.*

If you are in a conversation about a personal matter, an important business matter, a money matter, or the clarification of a misunderstanding, then the conversation has significance. You may not think you have as much skin in the game as the other party, but it is possible that you have as much to gain or lose without realizing it. None of us has a crystal ball or a prophet's insight, so it is best to be ready for all conversations headed our way. There is simply too much at stake *not* to be. Most conversations—if approached with awareness—are just another form of opportunity knocking.

Measuring Success in Conversation

Only the curious will learn . . . the quest quotient has always excited me more than the intelligence quotient.

— *Eugene Wilson*

Think back to your worst outcomes in conversation: the scenarios in which you really wanted something—maybe wanted some outcome too much—and everything went wrong. Unpleasant as the retrospect may be, there are important lessons to be learned regarding how and why conversations go awry and often backfire.

Years ago Mitch sat down for a significant conversation. He was a consultant to a start-up company and, at the time, felt that the founder (and CEO) was failing to recognize his contributions toward the company's growth. In the 18 months he had been directing the organization's marketing efforts, retail distribution had grown by more than 2,000 percent. And because he was working hard building the organization, he felt he should receive more positive feedback and compensation for his efforts.

In retrospect, Mitch realizes that he had been given a pretty fair deal for his contributions, including a generous part-time salary and 150,000 shares in a potential IPO. But at the time, he felt underappreciated and taken for granted—underscored by the fact that the company had burned through two marketing directors before him. His intention was to ask for a larger ownership share in the firm and asked the CEO a number of times for a meeting to discuss this proposal. The CEO kept finding creative maneuvers to avoid the conversation.

Not having much affinity for conversations with any potential for disagreement, this CEO instead preferred to keep such exchanges in a command-and-control arena, which only increased Mitch's frustration. Sensing that avoidance was the status quo, Mitch decided to put together a memo stating his views and offering increased involvement for increased compensation. There was no response to his memo for months—as if

Mitch had never written it; it seemed as if the CEO was fully committed to the avoid-dance.

Mitch pressed him for a sit-down and shortly discovered that this was mistake number two: you don't push individuals wired for autocracy to do anything. Mistake number one was requesting the conversation in the first place. As humbling as it was, Mitch sat and absorbed the CEO's wrath and reproof: "Are you serious about this request? Do you realize the ramifications of what you're asking for?"

"Let me illustrate what would happen to this company if I gave you what you want." He went on to illustrate on paper how he would have to do the same for all the other senior leaders in the organization and how his own stake in the enterprise would be diluted to a percentage that was unthinkable to him. "If I gave you what you want, imagine what the others would think and how it would affect the esprit de corps," he continued, and then went on to explain how such arrangements could poison an enterprise.

Mitch had grossly miscalculated the situation on two profound levels: (1) by focusing on his own contributions, he had underestimated the contributions of others, and (2) by focusing on his own desires, he had failed to grasp the impact of his request on the rest of the team. In this case, Mitch was the one who was self-focused and shortsighted.

The relational poison had been stewing in the CEO for months, and the arrangement disintegrated from there. The CEO no longer trusted Mitch, and Mitch no longer respected the CEO because of his avoidance methods. The lessons learned from this event were beneficial. Although agitated and riddled with angst at the time, Mitch embraced the need for recognizing the significance of others and the need for mutuality in a conversation. From the CEO's avoidance, he learned that there is little to be gained by refraining from important conversations, even if you feel the other party is wrong. But there is a way for handling such conversations that can end well for all involved.

"All good conversation is about learning and contains two elements: significance and mutuality."

— *Gordan Pask*

It is impossible to be truly objective in a conversation because we are there for our own intentions. The principal mistake we often make is overestimating our importance in the give and take, which leads to *underestimating* the other party's significance.

We often delude ourselves into thinking conversations are about getting what *we* want, when we want it. If these assumptions guide us in our conversations of significance, we are going to be disappointed. Conversations are, by definition, *about two or more parties walking away satisfied.*

You will thrive in the art of conversation if you grasp two principles: (1) the significance of the other party in the conversation and (2) that the conversation is about mutuality—"we" not "I."

In important conversations you either play the role of *initiator* or *responder.* Each role carries its own obligations. As an initiator, your primary responsibility is to do your best *to be understood.* As a responder, your primary responsibility is to do your best *to understand.* Great conversationalists remember their roles and meet their obligations, consequently multiplying their odds of truly connecting through conversation.

True north in conversation is located by being attuned to the magnetic polarity of *empathy*—understanding the significance of the other party in a particular

> *True north in conversation is located by being attuned to the magnetic polarity of empathy.*

conversation and achieving some level of mutuality at the conclusion. These outcomes are not possible if your intention in the exchange is to *instruct* rather than to *learn*. When you walk in as an instructor, you inevitably walk out frustrated at the lack of learning. When you walk in as a student, at the very least you will be satisfied at the illumination you gained into the person and the matter at hand.

There is an old saying about some teachers: "He says he has taught for 30 years, but he really taught for one year and repeated it 29 times." The same observation could be applied to the conversational style of many of the people we interact with daily. They could claim to have been in a thousand conversations, but in fact, have been repeating one conversation pattern over and over, ad nauseam. They are in the conversation to instruct—not to learn—and their instruction has grown stale. And so has their learning and development as human beings.

Conversations are significant because they can help us grow intellectually. Walking into a conversation as a student guided by curiosity promotes not only relational growth but also intellectual growth by virtue of synapse expansion—by being curious, we literally expand our gray matter. While conducting a study on curiosity and advertising discussed in his book *Curiosity Killed the Cat: Curiosity and Advertising,* Richard Taflinger came to the conclusion that "the greatest advantage of curiosity is the number of neurological connections it makes possible. Investigating the unusual and the unexplored paves new pathways in the brain. The more pathways we have, the more possible responses we have available to stimuli. The more possible responses we possess, the greater the likelihood of a proper response to another novel situation. Curiosity strengthens these learned responses."

By conversing with an open mind—and by truly listening—you can begin adding colors to your pallet, tools to your toolbox, compounds to your chemistry kit (choose your own metaphor). This openness will unleash the possibilities within you—and those around you.

Some of the people you meet during conversations have minds that are rock hard, sedentary, and static.

Others are like water—always flowing, searching for pathways, moving around, over, and through any opening that can be found. How you behave in conversations can, in fact, determine the breadth and depth of your intellectual expansion. If you settle into one pattern, that pattern will become your only playbook, and your potential for results will become predictably poor. But as you learn how to open up, listen, and identify the conversation for what it is, conversation becomes an expedition.

We are not yet who we will be. Our exchanges play a part in sculpting who we become. If others have something of value to add to us; if others are allowed to transmit ideas and concepts to our psyche; if we care to improve and evolve, then conversation becomes a _thigmotropism_—where we experience growth simply by being in contact with others and their ideas.

Every conversation has the potential to open up new neural pathways—highways of thought in our brains—leading to new possibilities and new connections in our lives. These highways impact our decision-making apparatus. It is not an exaggeration to say that approaching a conversation with curiosity could literally change our lives. Conversations are vital because they cause us to grow on the inside. And as our brains expand, so do our horizons and perspectives.

We succeed in conversation when we change our approach and perspective from an instructor to a student. This attitude literally causes our brains to grow new pathways through the act of conversing. We succeed when we aim for and settle for nothing less than significance for the other party and a spirit of mutuality.

Now we will explore the first point on the course of conversation, the all-important aspect of context and timing and its influence on conversation: why we are having this conversation at this particular moment, and how we can treat it with the proper respect.

> *We succeed in conversation when we change our approach and perspective from an instructor to a student.*

This Point in Time

Progress is not so much about time in conversation as it is timing in conversation.

—*Scott West and Mitch Anthony*

"Imagine your life as a movie that is just being 'shot,' but that you will not be permitted to 'cut' anything out of the original film. Once the film is taken it cannot be retroactively changed."[1]

Viktor Frankl used this analogy to help people when they were deciding how to act in a particular situation. By using this example, he sought to impress upon people the *irreversible quality* of human life and the historical nature of human existence.

---

[1] Viktor Frankl, *Man's Search for Meaning* (Boston: Beacon Press, 2006), 63.

To become a *master conversationalist*, your starting point is this principle: *Appreciate the singularity of each moment in your conversations*. Any moment in a conversation has an irreversible quality and historical importance in determining how that conversation will play out. How you respond to the conversation determines whether you will play protagonist or antagonist, hero or villain, supporting role, or find yourself on the cutting room floor.

To us, the point of conversation is like the needle on the compass of conversation pointing to the unique and irreversible singularity of each moment. Grasp the reality that this conversation—as it is at this moment—will never present itself in exactly the same way again. With this thought we are brought to the realization that the dynamic nature of events and people does not allow for repeat performances. We cannot flub our performance in a conversation and then demand a second take.

> *Grasp the reality that this conversation—as it is at this moment—will never present itself in exactly the same way again.*

Words that are said in the first take (constructive or destructive, thoughtful or flippant) will be woven into the fabric going forward. By the time we revisit the conversation, some critical dynamic will have changed, either in the emotions of the person involved or in the situation itself. A master conversationalist understands the critical role of timing in any discussion—because timing influences context, emotion, and openness. Consider the following examples we have encountered:

Terry, a business owner, shared his experience of sitting down with a business associate to discuss forming a partnership. Terry couldn't understand why the other person, who had become a friend, wasn't keen on the idea—until the friend started talking about his pending divorce. His friend and potential business partner had grown pessimistic about agreements and the overly optimistic promises that held them together. He was not in a place to enter any new agreements. Without knowledge of this key piece of context, Terry would have been offended and felt spurned; their working relationship would have suffered. Terry accepted the fact that timing was critical, and in this case, critically wrong.

This conversation was unwittingly and unintentionally ill-timed, and we would not have discovered that fact without a meaningful dialogue. The point in time for Terry's friend was a critical dynamic in the context of

Terry's offer. This story illustrates the importance of asking ourselves how the conversation we are advancing fits into the overall context of the other person's reality.

Mitch's 20-something son called to talk about whether or not he should change his career path and go back to school. Father and son were discussing possibilities when Mitch began to wonder why they were having this conversation at this moment—at this point in time. It occurred to him that his son had just been home for the holidays and had talked to a cousin around his same age who had just graduated from college and been accepted to law school. His cousin was quite enthused about all the prospects before him. Mitch's son, by comparison, felt like he was lagging in his own pursuits. By the time the conversation ended between Mitch and his son, his son realized that he could pursue a specific education to help broaden the scope of his original mission, which was to reach people who were suffering. A complete career change was not necessary.

This conversation was not so much about a new path in life as it was about affirming the path of service he had already chosen. The critical context was that his son was being torn between how society labels success and how he had chosen to use his talents and pursue his own dreams.

Conversations happen *when they happen* for a reason. Understanding the context and the specific timing is the first mission of the great conversationalist. You need to address a situation *as it is at the moment;* to do so, requires appreciating how you arrived at a particular point. If you are curious, you will want to know answers to the following questions:

- **"Why am I having this conversation right now and not a month ago, or a month from now?"**
- **"How did I get to where I am? What events or circumstances have led me to this conversation?"**
- **"How does this conversation fit into the bigger picture?"**
- **"Should I be having this conversation right now?"**

A heightened awareness comes with the realization that *this exact scenario will never repeat itself again*— an awareness that leads to a raised esteem for what someone is saying and why. Does he feel the situation has gone too far, or is he trying to prevent something worse from developing? Is he worried, offended, hurt, or fed up? Does he see this situation as an indicator of future developments? The answers to these important questions are impossible to understand without hearing the contextual story that led up to this particular conversation. *You cannot discover the fruits of conversation until you first find the roots of conversation.*

There are two timelines at play in every situation— one *chronological* and the other *visceral*. Both contexts are important in determining where you are at in a particular conversation. The chronological timeline helps you understand the backdrop to the story, while the visceral timeline helps you understand the other party in terms of emotion invested and emotion spent. Intuitively you will want to ask yourself if this conversation is happening at an emotional peak or nadir. If you are too early or too late on the visceral timeline, you will not get the result you hoped for.

Scott can think of no more significant conversations in his life than those he engaged in as part of his recovery from alcohol addiction. As part of the recovery process, he was encouraged to make direct amends to those people in the past who have suffered as a result of his behavior.

In these difficult but crucial encounters, Scott teetered between two conflicting desires that are common to the initiator of an important, but difficult conversation:

1. _Delay_ **for as long as possible, hoping the dialogue becomes unnecessary with the passing of time.**
2. _Rush_ **the appointment, in large part because of a personal desire for catharsis.**

In reality, sensitivity to the emotional condition of the other party—_at a specific point in time_—must be the singular consideration for attaining even a reasonable probability for success in that conversation. Early contact with a fresh wound can only intensify the pain and delay the healing. On the other hand, without any attention, the wound will harden and scar, preventing any further opportunity for healing. Scott's best results came when he focused on the context of _appropriate timing for the other party._

Understanding the contextual story and the emotional need of the other party constitutes your safety vest as you enter the waters of turbulent conversation. If a conversation revolves around some form of injury, disagreement, negotiation, or injury, it becomes vital to guide your sense of curiosity toward comprehending the other person's context, story, and emotional need. You will rarely misstep in a conversation if you do so.

Pascal remarked that the branch can never grasp the meaning of the whole tree. Assume the tree represents the sum of your life and what it will become, and each branch represents your important and pivotal conversations. The fruit harvested from these branches are the resulting gains in relationships and outcomes from each conversation. It may be helpful to envision your next important conversation as a branch on your own tree of life.

The master conversationalist disciplines himself to be **fully present** *in each conversation.*

The master conversationalist disciplines himself to be *fully present* in each conversation. Being fully present begins with a curiosity around the genealogy leading to the particular conversation: "Why am I here right now? What led me to this point?"

When playing the role of responder in an important conversation, you might say, "This feels really important—you must have given this a lot of thought." This response may flush out the timing aspect of the conversation and indicate where this particular conversation fits into the larger scheme of things in the initiator's mind.

What you hear will help you determine exactly where the other party is at in terms of events and emotions.

Understanding this context creates a layer of appreciation and consciousness, enabling you to bring a more palatable sense of meaning to your conversations, as well as a sense of personal importance to the other party.

Ask yourself how your next conversation fits into the larger picture of that person's life and well-being, as well as your own. By doing your best to capture the meaning of the moment, you will discover the first point of conversation—timing and context, and the fact that this moment can never again repeat itself. This understanding naturally and gracefully moves you toward the second point on the course of conversation—*understanding the other person's point of view.*

I See Your Point

A traveler asks a farmer how to get to a particular village. The farmer replies, "If I were you, I wouldn't start from here. . . ."

—*Anonymous*

Many would say that as a culture we are not growing in our understanding of others. With the aid of the partisan media, we are being squeezed into pigeonholes of perspective. If you are a conservative, you watch Fox News exclusively and affirm your views nightly. If you are a liberal, you watch MSNBC (or Jon Stewart on Comedy Central) and do the same.

If you are driving in your SUV, you program yourself with AM talk radio. If you are driving your hybrid, you program yourself with NPR. Millions of us are being molded by the monomedia effect. We no longer have a need for expanding our point of view—only for shining, buffing, and embellishing our current views.

We are well past the time for questioning whether or not this approach toward shaping our views is helping us to become better communicators or better conversationalists. The argument could be made that this style of conditioning is nudging us toward laziness—where conversations are exercises in verbal futility. We don't need to listen or think about what we are hearing when we can simply parrot what we've been programmed to say. There's no need to understand or examine our views because they are set, static, and complete.

Perhaps it was the resulting cultural tendentiousness of this trend that led Cal Thomas and Bob Beckel to write the book, *Common Ground: How to Stop the Partisan War That Is Destroying America*. The authors sniffed out the cultural default toward eristic debate so finely argumentative that it is resulting in a downward spiral of redundancy in dialogue, regardless of the topic. We give the same response over and over because we are programmed to think and talk in a certain manner from a very certain perspective.

Cal Thomas is a conservative columnist and Bob Beckel is a liberal strategist. These longtime friends are often able to find common ground on issues that lawmakers in Washington cannot seem to locate. Their approach to dialogue is a breath of fresh air in an age of opinionated entrenchment. Their syndicated columns appear on opinion pages across the United States. The format is a template for how we can and should enter conversation on any topic where emotion is invested. The first two-thirds of their column explains their point of view (POV) without condescension or insult, while the final third is dedicated to finding points they can both agree on, despite their POVs.

How is it that Thomas and Beckel are able to converse so elegantly? It is only because they are friends first. It is clear that their conversations are grounded in respect and dignity. Although they see the world through separate lenses, one can sense that they are curious about how each other's mind works. The result is the ability to locate planks of commonality with which they can build some form of agreement. They understand the power of perspective and how it is shaped.

We offer this example because we see the tenor and tendency of political conversations bleeding into our general patterns of conversation. If we cannot shift our gears of comprehension into neutral long enough to actually hear the other person's perspective, then true conversation runs the risk of becoming an endangered practice.

Thomas and Beckel's example is pointing us toward a solution for the dearth of genuine conversation in our lives. In an effort to get our point across—because we want to make our point so badly—we often cannot hear or comprehend responses. The solution is evident: In conversation you need to behave in a manner that convinces the other party of your desire to truly *hear* his or her point of view.

> *If we cannot shift our gears of comprehension into neutral long enough to actually hear the other person's perspective, then true conversation runs the risk of becoming an endangered practice.*

Edward DeBono, one of the world's great authorities on human thinking processes, stated that in western civilizations we have a dichotomous, preset approach to matters: "You state your view, and I'll take the other side." The consequence is that in our attempts to converse or exchange ideas, we often get trapped in *either/or exchanges* that bear little fruit but collect plenty of thorns.

Until the other party in the conversation is convinced that you sincerely want to hear her perspective and understand her view, she will be preoccupied with sharpening her own blade, striking the greatest blow, and winning the debate. Winning a debate is, at best, an oxymoron.

When you introduce civility as your conversational platform, a civility built from dignified respect and genuine curiosity, the spirit of the exchange is immediately and deeply affected. Hopefully you have witnessed the phenomenon of civil and respectful conversation—when both parties are convinced of the other's desire to hear and understand, and the exchange literally becomes a contest of courtesy:

- **"Go ahead. I want to hear what you think."**
- **"Please, tell me your view."**
- **"I insist. I really want to know what you're thinking here."**

Now you can enter the exchange without defenses. Your fears of attack or accusation are disarmed. You become open to hearing the other party and reaching a place of mutuality. Civility is a cornerstone for successful conversation, which is expressed best in tone, body language, and posture.

Civility and mutuality can also be introduced into a conversation simply by altering the geometry of the conversation. Scott has noted that if two people are talking about a problem and there is a piece of paper representing the problem situated *between* them, this placement often impedes the resolution process because the matter is physically situated between them.

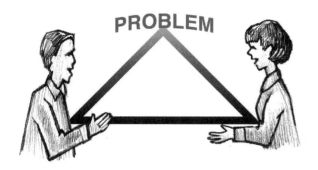

By forming a triangle where the paper representing the problem is placed *outside* of the two people in the exchange, a spirit of mutuality—of wanting to solve the problem—now enters the conversation. This setup helps dissipate the tension between the parties engaged in the conversation. In this case, the triangle is the preferred geometric alignment.

Years ago Mitch conducted leadership workshops with student groups in schools. The goal was to find agreement among leaders of various student groups and come up with solutions to issues facing the schools. He would begin the workshop by asking, "Do you think that the way you are *situated* in this conversation will have any impact on the results you get today?" The room was always set up as a traditional classroom with all chairs facing the front.

Mitch would then announce, "I am leaving the room to let you think about this question, and I'll return in seven minutes to see what conversational geometry you have decided upon for achieving the best results."

Groups inevitably came up with a single pattern— a circle. When asked why they chose the circle, they would reply, "Because in a circle we can look each other in the eye. We're all at the same status, and we all matter."

Cliquish gatherings and the resulting views and tension with other cliques serve as a good analogy for what ails our society. The conversation must move beyond the preconceived stereotypes of groups and individuals before we can make progress.

One of Mitch's sons, who readily admits to being born with an argumentative nature, told Mitch of an exercise he was forced to endure in a social studies class. The teacher handed out a list of inflammatory social issues and instructed each student to take a position on the topics. After taking their position, the students were then instructed to build an argument for the opposing point of view. After the expected objections, both moral and intellectual, the students began mining views they had never before dared to consider. Being forced to build an argument on behalf of a view they found offensive stretched their capacity for thinking, understanding, and civility.

It was not only a mind-expanding exercise for the students but also an epiphany regarding POV; namely, that people have very good reasons—experience and observations stacked together—that influence the color and hue of their views. The fact that an individual does not sympathize with those views should not prevent that person from comprehending or attempting to understand another person's POV. If nothing else, this shift in attitude demonstrates respect for the other party in the conversation.

Mitch's son took to the exercise with relish and is now able to converse in controversial arenas. Mitch had to scratch his head as his son sat up at night formulating arguments for legalizing prostitution, drug use, and other libertarian arguments. Mitch asked his son, "Do you really believe that?"

"Of course not," his son replied. "But it helps to understand the people who do." It was about learning to disagree without being disagreeable.

And that, after all, is the point of conversation, a point we should strive to never lose sight of. Dignity, respect, and civility are the result—when they are the foundation for engaging in dialogue.

⸻

It is never easy to pull our egos out of their need to say what they have to say—to express our point of view. Our obsession with airing our own views eventually causes conversations to devolve into presentations, arguments, and sometimes something much worse.

Mitch and his wife recently experienced a POV epiphany over a recurring conversation regarding the amount of time their son was spending playing online games. A tension had been slowly building between mom, dad, and son. Mitch wanted less time spent on the games, with more adherence to time limits. Mitch's wife defended their son's position, feeling that their son was being harassed needlessly. Mitch felt that he was being sabotaged, and his wife felt that she was being unfairly accused of advocating an online obsession.

There were plenty of messages being sent—with little

> *Our obsession with airing our own views eventually causes conversations to devolve into presentations, arguments, and sometimes something much worse.*

progress. Mitch and his wife decided to communicate their respective points of view. Mitch articulated that, from his point of view, it was about discipline and life-style balance. He wanted their son to get more physical exercise and face-to-face social interaction instead of sitting in front of a computer. Mitch wanted him to practice discipline in terms of keeping preset time limits.

From his wife's point of view, it was about affirmation and social connectivity. She felt that Mitch's constant badgering was making their son feel that his interests were inferior, and that if he had spent the same amount of time doing some traditional activity like basketball, it would not have been an issue. Social connectivity came into the equation because their son's friends were playing this online game at the same time and were "meeting each other" in this virtual arena.

Discipline or affirmation. Which is more important?

Balance or social connectivity. Which matters more?

It all depends on your point of view, doesn't it?

Once the two POVs were vetted (with respect) and both points were taken into consideration, they were able to reach a more genuine agreement. Authentic consideration of the other party's point of view is the starting point of fruitful conversation.

When you sit down to converse—having already resolved that the other person will leave the conversation with satisfaction—the natural result is the ability to hear and see from his or her point of view:

- **"How do you see this situation?"**
- **"What is your perspective on what is happening?"**

Great conversationalists know that a point of understanding cannot be reached until you broaden your perspective to see the situation from someone else's vantage point, thus expanding your own point of view.

Once you are determined to truly understand where the other party is coming from, you are in a better position to make contact in a real and meaningful way. In the next chapter, we'll talk about the two *points of contact* that cause conversations to click or crash.

Making Contact at the Point of Conversation

If you insist on sticking to the facts, the facts won't stick.

—*Scott West*

It's a cold winter day. The temperature is −15° with a windchill of −35°. Your vehicle is outside exposed to the frigid north wind. When you attempt to start your vehicle, you hear nothing—not a crank, not a turn, not even a whine.

You brave the elements and try to flag down someone who might have jumper cables. Potential Good Samaritans look at you like you're asking them to build a car from scratch. Fortune smiles at you and someone stops, eager to help. Although relieved to finally have some assistance, you are slightly worried that—given the harsh elements—your helper could execute the task sloppily.

Anyone who has jumped a battery knows the risks. There are two points of contact necessary to bring it to life. If there is corrosion on a post, you are going to hear lifeless moaning. If the connections get crossed, you are going to hear an explosion or see a fire. It is not a task to be taken lightly.

Our conversations possess a similar dynamic. In dialogue there are two posts of connection necessary to jump-start a conversation. If we miss one of the connections, the result is *conversation DOA*. If we cross the connections, the result is *conversation TNT*. If we succeed in establishing contact with the polarities of both posts, the result is the transfer of energy—a positive experience for all involved.

> *In dialogue there are two posts of connection necessary to jump-start a conversation. If we miss one of the connections, the result is* conversation DOA. *If we cross the connections, the result is* conversation TNT.

What happens when you have a defining conversation? Can you remember a time when you walked away from an exchange feeling the power and energy flowing between the two of you? Here's what actually happened: You had a conversation where you experienced a clean connection with both sides of the brain—you were connected with the two posts. The proper transfer of energy requires the right connection.

We're going to ask and hopefully answer two important questions about *connectivity in the realm of conversation:*

1. **What manner of approach is required in order to avoid the sluggish response (DOA) or the volatile reaction (TNT)?**
2. **What are the posts—or points—of connection in the art of conversation?**

The two terminals requiring contact in conversation are the *outward* (what's happening) and the *inward* (emotional and conceptual). They require two distinct signals to connect. The outward post is looking for facts, accurate descriptions, agendas, and results. The inward post is looking for context, symmetry, understanding, and empathy. If we could advertise specifically what we are promising to deliver in conversations, it would be progress and understanding:

Progress: "You'll get what you need."
Understanding: "I get it. I get you."

Let's dig deeper and begin exploring the necessary steps for developing a more effective contact between both posts in our conversations.

Outward (Progress)

The outward post of conversation represents demonstrating competence and gaining command of both the facts and the situation. We need to demonstrate our intent to follow through so that progress can be made. People feel energy if they get the signal that the following can—and will—happen:

- **Progress will be made in the short term (the acute or immediate need).**
- **Progress will be made in the long term (the source of the issue).**

To aid cognizance of the two posts of conversation, we like to use the expressions "in-words" and "out-words."

Each party has an inward and an outward agenda that is being addressed by word, tone, and authenticity. *Out-words* refer to words and conversation concerning the outward agenda. *In-words* refer to words and conversation concerning the inward agenda.

Here are examples of "outward post" questions people ponder during a conversation:

Out-words:
> What exactly is the issue here?
> Who did what?
> Who wants what?
> What is at stake?
> Is this a reasonable request?
> What will it take to get this done?

Along with satisfying the outward need for a display of competence and the need for progress being made, we simultaneously satisfy the inward post's more visceral needs.

Inward (Understanding)

The inward post of conversation is about demonstrating empathy—by absorbing the other person's story and understanding his or her feelings. People feel energy if they receive these signals from you:

- **You understand the situation.**
- **You understand their sentiments about the situation.**

Here are examples of the "inward post" questions people ponder during a conversation:

In-words:

What is the story here?

What is the backdrop of this situation?

How does this tie into other issues I'm aware of?

Whose egos and feelings are on the line?

Who is affected by this, and how?

Am I being heard and respected for my views?

We can ensure satisfaction for both conversational polarities by remembering that there are two distinct agendas that need to be satisfied, outward and inward. Great conversationalists gather more than facts—they gather the driving spirit of the conversation.

The predominant concern with conversationalists who are outwardly focused is their concern with *what is going to happen.* Their focal point is the *outward* steps and action points that effect a tangible result. These are the individuals you've met who are magnetized to the phrase, "What are our next steps?" Their power is drawn from the outward post meeting the outward agenda. If someone tries to offer input on how this idea might rub someone the wrong way, this person may discount this input as irrelevant and ask again, "So what steps will we take?"

Conversationalists who are inwardly focused keep pushing back to the *concept,* trying to gain clarity about the idea because conceptually it doesn't feel quite right. They're hesitant as to how well this concept will *integrate* with what already exists.

There are people who are concerned with how to *navigate through egos and emotions.* They just want to make sure their views are *understood.* Concept, integration, emotional navigation, empathy, and respect are all functions involving the inward post of emotion. If these issues are not addressed, the power stops flowing to the inward post.

Quite often in conversations the outward agenda is given preeminence. *In-words* are easily discounted by phrases such as, "Let's just stick to the facts." In these situations, one individual's sentiments and ideas regarding the matter are secondary to what the other individual perceives to be the facts.

What fact-harnessed people fail to realize is that emotions *are* facts. What is more real to us than how we feel about certain people or situations? Emotions become facts of life! They become so real that we could call them *emotional facts*. Not only is understanding and empathizing with the emotional aspect of a matter important, recent research indicates that focusing on the emotional side of the discussion can help retain factual aspects as well.

> *Not only is understanding and empathizing with the emotional aspect of a matter important . . . focusing on the emotional side of the discussion can help retain factual aspects as well.*

Neuroscience tells us we don't remember facts unless they are associated with emotion. The human eye picks up one trillion pixels of information each day but forgets the flowers by the road, the 300 advertisements we're exposed to, and the buildings we pass—unless there is an emotion attached to the picture. Data without emotion doesn't register in our long-term memory.

Emotional experiences and events—those emotional facts we just talked about—can be fragile and take time to completely set into memory. Known as *consolidation,* this allows emotions to influence the way memories are stored.

The amygdala is the part of our brain that is associated with fear and aggression, which is critical for visual learning and memory. The amygdala is responsible for *memory consolidation* (also known as *memory modulation*), the process of transferring information from your "working" memory to "long-term" memory. Research has shown that the greater the level of emotional arousal at the time of the event, the greater the chance that the event will be remembered.[2] A good example of this is the conversation you have that centers around, "Do you remember where you were?" when a major event occurred. The emotional impact was so great that you

[2]For example, see M.A. Conway and C.W. Pearce Pleydell, "The Construction of Autobiographical Memories in the Self Memory System," *Psychological Review* 107 (2000): 261.

instantly remember where you were, as well as numerous other details you may not have otherwise remembered.

Scott works with an investment company that studied the impact of emotions on conversation. They found that there was a definite fact/emotion dynamic in defining conversations. The group conducted one-on-one dialogues with investors, ages 45–69, with investable assets of $250,000 to $1 million. The investors held a variety of technical and nontechnical occupations.

Interviewers had two conversations with each investor, each of which presented the same set of facts. One conversation emphasized emotion and empathy, while the other reduced the role of emotion and focused on just the facts.

Every participant preferred the emotion-based conversation over the fact-based one, and all were more open to new information. In the debriefings following the two conversations, every participant reported that the emotion-based conversations included more data and information, even though both conversations contained identical data.

Personal agreement was a key emotional element of the conversation. By adding an empathetic statement that the advisor felt the same way as the investor, the investor felt his interests were aligned and that he was being heard. All data that followed in the conversation had a higher recall rate than data that was not preceded by personal agreement.

When people enter into conversations where they want to motivate or sway another person, they tend to focus just on facts and become frustrated when they fail to come to an agreement. But a defining conversation takes place by making contact with both posts of conversation—factual and emotional—resulting in mutuality and a higher likelihood that progress is being made.

Emotional facts contribute to why people leave companies, marriages, and friendships—and why people decline to get excited or buy into an idea. If we find our relevant emotions in a matter being dismissed, it becomes a defining context for our decisions going forward. Many personal and professional failures are found in the wake of dismissing emotional facts.

Far too often in conversation, how a person feels about the situation is treated as meaningless or trite. In business and in life, respecting and understanding a person's sentiments represents the spinal column of a successful relationship.

By attending to both the inward and outward aspects of a conversation, we validate the individual and bolster his or her confidence in the processes we employ for success. We communicate that we get the gist of the conversation, which is simultaneously factual and emotional in nature.

Once we truly understand the transfer of energy between posts in our conversations, we can commit to helping people walk away satisfied on both agendas: progress and understanding. Because we are cognizant about meeting their inward agenda—even if we don't come to an agreement—we at least know that others can walk away knowing they have been heard. For most of us, satisfying the inward agenda is rewarding, given the levels of self-absorption permeating our culture.

In your next conversation, commit to making both points of connection. With that commitment you will be vigilant toward comprehending both outward and inward agendas. You accomplish this by clearly understanding (1) the progress that needs to be made and (2) the backdrop story/emotions that are driving the conversation. Be aware as a listener that the *out-words* agenda is understood with what, when, where, and who questions, while the *in-words* agenda is understood with how, who, and why questions.

The concept of making two magnetic polarities work in conversation is simple to remember. Great conversations, like great relationships, are the result of ensuring proper connections. When you succeed at gathering power on both posts of conversation, you can look the other person in the eye and truthfully say, *"I get it, now let's get it done."* This is the difference between ordinary and defining conversations.

Now that you understand how to conduct a defining conversation, let's get back to the reality that most of us live with: dealing with those people who don't get it—and the counterfeit forms of conversation they use. The skill of making real contact through conversation is a goal that comes with impediments. We are constantly being challenged by conversation saboteurs who have supplanted the point of conversation with gamesmanship. These are the individuals who are looking to control, divide, and dominate any conversational exchange they enter. In the next chapter, we will learn how to recognize their tactics and discover ways to both disarm and defuse them.

Monologues and Dialogues: How to Identify a Conversation Saboteur

In conversation, it is best to walk in someone's shoes before you talk about his views.

— *Scott West and Mitch Anthony*

The Pony Express rider pulled up on his haggard-looking horse covered in dust from head to toe. He handed a letter to John Settler in Denver, Colorado. "What is this all about?" John asked.

The rider responded with, "I don't know and I don't rightly care either. I just rode 851 miles through peril and plain from St. Louis to here, to deliver this here message and I'm not in the least bit concerned with you liking what you've read. I've done my job and will be on my way."

"But," John Settler said, "I don't recognize the name on this letter."

"Neither do I," said the rider, "but that's for you to figure out, not me." And off to the east he rode.

Very often when we think we are entering into a conversation, we are flummoxed to learn that, in fact, we are not there to be heard or understood. We are there to be told something, presented to, or controlled—to be *messaged* in one form or another. The people doing the messaging come in many shapes, sizes, and caricatures, and we are challenged to communicate with them on a weekly, if not daily basis. Like the Pony Express rider, these people are there to deliver a package and then head home—not to converse. If you don't like the message, that's your problem.

And why do most of us loathe going to meetings to partake in group "conversations"? In part, because so much gets said and so little gets done. We labor through these discussions and wonder how in the world we survived before the Blackberry® was invented.

One undeniable factor impeding progress in conversations is that certain, but identifiable saboteurs supplant the point of conversation with counterfeits. In this chapter, we will reveal the saboteurs, and in the next chapter, we will reveal the counterfeit forms that are often substituted for real conversations. To lay the foundation for what does and does not constitute conversation, it is important to distinguish between a dialogue and a monologue.

A simple method for illustrating the difference is to draw upon the words' origins. Both words are derived from the Greek roots *mono logos* (one meaning) and *dia logos* (the merging of meaning). Monologists enter a conversation for the purpose of getting their point across. Monologists are readily identified by their tones, whether they are dominant, argumentative, condescending, entertaining, or droning. Monologists are not present to hear your point; they are in the room to prove their own points or to simply dominate airtime.

We acknowledge that it is human nature to predict a predicament and premeditate a response. It is also human nature to want to defend your own point of view. But it is the lower form of human nature to fail to see past your own nose. Monologists more often than not capitulate to this nature.

Dialogists, on the other hand, first attempt to understand your meaning and then search for a way to merge their point *and* yours. The dialogist's approach hearkens back to the idea that mutuality, along with significance, are the true goalposts of conversation.

In many ways, a dialogue is akin to assembling a puzzle from the pieces—some that come from you, and some that come from the other person in the conversation. You know what your pieces are made of and can only assume to know what the other person's pieces are. The purpose of a dialogue is to discover what the other party's puzzle pieces look like and how and where they merge with your ideas.

Many meetings and conversations, instead of functioning as dialogues, end up being more like open-mic night at the Improv. People prepare their material and look for acknowledgment and approval for what they bring. When you enter into dialogues, you must ask yourself whether you are present just to say your piece or to put all the pieces together. Monologues reflect personal interest. Dialogues reflect interest in another person.

> *Many meetings and conversations, instead of functioning as dialogues, end up being more like open-mike night at the Improv.*

Below are the definitions of the word *monologue*. Do these remind you of behavior you have witnessed in conversation?

mon·o·logue[3]

1. A long passage in a play or motion picture spoken by one actor, or an entire play for one actor only
2. A long tedious uninterrupted speech during a conversation
3. A set of jokes or humorous stories following one another without a break, told by a solo entertainer

Owing to the dearth of skilled dialogists among us, conversations often evolve into fencing or jousting contests between various types of monologists. It has been said that, as a culture, we are amusing ourselves to death. When observing conversations in our culture, we could say that we are not only amusing ourselves to death but also controlling ourselves to death. This is especially observable in a group conversation, where some participants are there to attract attention and others to control.

Monologists, like actors on a stage, are primarily concerned with delivering their own lines and winning approval and attention. We are betting you'll recognize some of the following types of conversation saboteurs.

---

[3] Encarta® World English Dictionary © 1999.

Talk Show Host

You will never have a real conversation with the talk show host. These individuals will cut you off at their whim and continue their monologue. With little or no prompting, they will wrestle away the microphone and never give it back. The talk show hosts are the individuals whose voice acts like a generator to their vocal chords—supplying energy that increases the charge as they talk. The more they talk, the louder they get. Talk show hosts never really engage in dialogue because they view conversation as an opportunity to have an audience. It soon becomes apparent that they like the sound of their voice. They try to make a point but it evolves into a soliloquy. They can't stop themselves—it's simply too soothing for them to hear their own voice.

Graffiti Artist

Graffiti artists are the individuals who are unable to prevent themselves from marring or distracting from another person's message with their own artistic expressions, which often take the form of entertainment or artistry. They often view the conversation as a platform for their wit. They either act out of innocent intent or a more sinister attempt to distract or derail the conversation. The end effect is the obscuring or defacing of the central message that matters in a dialogue. Graffiti artists sometimes stake out territory with their artsy clichés and need to push the boundaries while entertaining themselves with minimal regard for the original intent of the conversation. The flow of any conversation becomes increasingly unrecognizable as these individuals express their work.

Some graffiti artists are talented, witty, and fun to listen to: why else would they have been invited into the conversation? These people, however, denigrate the process by relentlessly bringing attention back to themselves.

Sir Edmund Hillary (Mountain Climber)

These skilled conversationalists always have a better story than you—they've always climbed a higher mountain: "Jim, that's a great story you told about climbing Mt. Kilimanjaro. It reminds me of something that happened to me the fifth time I reached the peak of Everest . . . I'd done it solo and was so exhausted . . ." Blah, blah, blah.

Mountain climbers are the individuals who have inhaled the idea that their experiences are more important and more instructive than anyone else's experiences and ideas. More than likely they are driven by their insecurities that someone else may have had an experience more vibrant than their own.

Psychic

 Believing themselves to be clairvoyant regarding what others are thinking, psychics habitually jump in during the middle of your thought and finish it for you. Or believing themselves to be superior thinkers, they jump in before you can further demonstrate your paucity of intelligence, thus saving you from yourself—at least in their minds. We suspect that many psychics are battling an internal energy issue where they struggle to contain their impulse to interrupt or respond, or they have an inflated ego (or maybe both). They have an internal clock ticking away and when the alarm goes off, they need to be heard again: "It's been a full half-minute and I haven't been heard from." Either way, the psychic's habit of *conversatus interruptus* exasperates all involved.

Ultimate Fighter

Laying in the bush waiting for the wrong thing to be said, a naïve suggestion to surface, or an idea to get floated that is well within the range of their weapons of pessi-
mism and scorn, ultimate fighters ambush the conversation process with negativity and cynical clichés:

> "Where have we heard that one before?"
> "Oh, sure. Yeah, that'll work."
> "Maybe we should pay attention to what happened the last time we had this conversation."
> "Prove it!"

Ultimate fighters are never short on poison arrows. Their role requires little intellectual rigor or creativity. They simply watch the radar for suggestions and then shoot them down like they are playing a game of conversational Galaga.

Ultimate fighters are those intense individuals who are agenda- and ego-driven combatants in conversation. They view each conversation as a competition with a clear winner and clear loser. Make a move and they will counter it immediately. They are not satisfied until they get you to tap out and surrender completely to their agenda.

Ultimate fighters are often masters of laconic and abrupt replies—whatever your thought may be, it's not good enough. They have their assumptions and are not interested in your thoughts or ideas. They are smarter and more seasoned than you, and their minds are made up before the conversation has begun. Being combative in nature, ultimate fighters habitually miss the point of conversation in an effort to win another round.

Parachutist

 Have you ever had a conversation with someone where you were scratching your head and asking yourself, "Where is this person coming from?" These are the individuals who drop in on a conversation, unannounced and uninvited. Parachutists assume their input is wanted and needed. Feeling strongly about themselves and their input, parachutists presume that there is always a global demand for their opinions. When engaging in significant conversations, keep an eye out for parachutists showing up in no-fly zones.

A parachutist is often a third party showing up uninvited but can also appear in a two-person conversation where one party shows up ill-prepared for the conversation at hand. This individual is parachuting in by virtue of either not having anything relevant to add or unaware of the context of the conversation.

Allowing that this cast of characters can sabotage any meaningful conversation at any moment, there arises a need for authentic participants in the process—participants who understand why we are having a conversation and allow others to share the space. Dialogists understand that conversation is a space where things need to happen and people need to know

Dialogists understand that conversation is a space where things need to happen and people need to know that they matter.

that they matter. Progress and significance are the goals.

In order to keep the saboteurs at bay, dialogists intentionally need to put the *quest* back into the question and *convergence* back into the conversation. Before you can become a standout dialogist, you'll need to come to a better understanding of the counterfeit forms of conversation and discover methods for exposing and subduing those forms.

CHAPTER NINE

Sold, Told, Put On Hold: How to Detect a Counterfeit Conversation

A person can sound really good but actually have nothing to say.

— *Scott West and Mitch Anthony*

Can you recall a conversation where you really wanted to make a connection, but instead walked away feeling angry, frustrated, or discouraged? You most likely encountered a person who could not hear anything you were saying, although he went through the charade of conversing with you, even though his mind was already made up. The person was not there to hear you, understand you, or meet you halfway—he was there to *convince* you. Period. End of conversation.

You've been in enough important conversations to know how rare it is to make an authentic connection. A reason for this lack of connectivity is that far too often people come into conversations with agendas other than finding out what you need and are hoping to deliver.

When people want to communicate with one another, they have an abundance of techniques to choose from—some effective and some counterproductive. Look at the following list of communication modalities and rank them from 1–10, 1 being the least effective and 10 the most:

- ___ **Messaging**
- ___ **Advising**
- ___ **Selling**
- ___ **Avoiding**
- ___ **Conversing**
- ___ **Arguing**
- ___ **Reprimanding**
- ___ **Inquiring**
- ___ **Debating**
- ___ **Telling**

Although there is no absolute right answer, we have found that most people would arrange the top three modes as *conversing, inquiring,* and *advising. Selling, arguing, avoiding* and *reprimanding* generally end up near the bottom (unless the respondent is a sales professional), and *debating, telling,* and *messaging* fall somewhere in the middle.

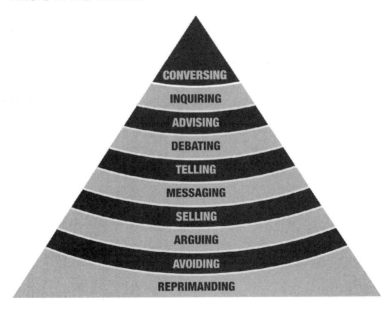

CONVERSING

INQUIRING

ADVISING

DEBATING

TELLING

MESSAGING

SELLING

ARGUING

AVOIDING

REPRIMANDING

The preferred mode of communication is contingent on the situation at hand. People don't mind a healthy debate but they generally don't like to engage in an argument where their point of view is discounted. People don't mind being advised when they are seeking advice, but they are put off by the technique when they are seeking a conversation instead. There is a time for *messaging*. We all recognize that there are situations where *telling* (presenting is a form of this mode), *selling,* or *inquiring* are the appropriate responses. There is even a time and place for *reprimanding* or *avoiding* a conversation.

Problems most often arise around the need for conversation. We require conversation in many situations where we instead are greeted with inappropriate substitutes such as *selling, telling, arguing, avoiding,* and *reprimanding.* These substitutes only serve to further frustrate the situation that is begging for genuine conversation. By virtue of being applied at the wrong time and in the wrong place, these techniques have become nothing more than counterfeit forms of conversation.

Conversation and inquiry stand at the top of the communication hierarchy because these methods lend themselves toward achieving mutuality more than any others. Conversation and inquiry are forms of communication where we are looking to *learn* something and then to integrate what we learn into a dialogue. All the other communication techniques available to us are forms of proving, telling, or avoiding.

If you do not understand that the true nature of conversation is the *merging of meanings*, your own meaning takes precedence and you revert to monologue tactics. Odds are, instead of a dialogue, you are more likely to encounter the following communication maneuvers, which we refer to as *counterfeit conversations:*

- **Being sold**
- **Being told**
- **Being put on hold**

The highest order of exchange available to us as humans is the conversation. You need to be careful not to allow counterfeiters to depreciate the value of truly engaging in dialogue. To prevent these counterfeiting phenomena from eroding your conversations, you need to be aware of the forgeries and become adept in arresting them when they come into play.

The highest order of exchange available to us as humans is the conversation.

People who do not comprehend a defining conversation tend to see the exchange as an opportunity for persuasion—for getting what they want. With some people's attempts at persuasion, we can assume a degree of innocence because they may be acting out of their best intentions and are simply ignorant of the higher threshold of conversation available to them. We refer to these types as *unwitting counterfeiters.* However, in the case of the *willing counterfeiters,* manipulation is the motive, and the objective is to work the conversation toward their own benefit. Let's take a look at the most common conversation counterfeits, both unwitting and willing.

SOLD

Unwitting Sellers

These individuals really are excited about their point of view or experience and want to share it with others. They hope that by selling you on their point of view, you will experience their same level of enthusiasm.

Willful Sellers

The point here is to convince you of something other than what you want by making a case for their idea. Willful sellers often use fear, uncertainty, and doubt to further their cause. With these types of counterfeiters, there's a chance that their ideas are right—but they primarily tend to be pushy, unrelenting personality types who are cunningly persuasive. They know they can break you down through importunity and use this method to stay in control of both people and situations.

TOLD

Unwitting Tellers

These individuals have done their homework and are trying to save you the trouble of making a misguided decision. They are attempting to be rational, measured, and careful—and may truly have your best interests at heart.

Willful Tellers

The point of these counterfeiters is to convince you that you are wrong and they are right. This can be done overtly, as in "You've got it wrong," or covertly, as in "Let me tell you what's really happening." The latter response is designed to insinuate that you don't know what you're talking about. Willful tellers are typically black-and-white thinkers who tend to assume defensive postures in conversation. Their general posture and tone seem to say, "If you really knew what you were talking about, you wouldn't have said that."

PUT ON HOLD

Unwitting Avoiders

These individuals really don't want to make a mistake. They don't like to commit without much contemplation. Unwitting avoiders could be at a place where they are not yet convinced, or they could be the kind of individuals who just are not comfortable taking a position on any matter infused with emotion.

Willful Avoiders

The point of this counterfeit is to convince you that they are going to walk away from this conversation and *do something*—when they have absolutely no intention of doing any such thing. These specious stall tactics imitate the language of the doer, minus the intentionality:

> "Let me look into that and get back to you."
> "I'll have a conversation with so and so and we'll take it from there."

"Let's see how things play out in the next few weeks and continue this conversation then."

These put-on-hold lines may sound somewhat promising until you realize that you're being strung along because this person doesn't want to deal with your issue, is incapable of dealing with your issue, or doesn't agree with you but is unwilling to say so.

Delayers or avoiders can be passive-aggressive and noncommittal (people who just have a hard time deciding), or CMB-minded individuals (cover my booty) who simply don't want to be responsible for something if is doesn't work out.

The unwitting delayers have learned that if they keep putting you off, you eventually will get distracted by other matters and forget about them. They use these human foibles to their full benefit.

It takes two to have a conversation. If two people are not participating, conversations become an

It takes two to have a conversation.

exercise in futility. We believe that when you recognize a counterfeit conversation or conversation counterfeiter, you can diplomatically steer the conversation back toward a dialogue where two people are not only talking but also listening and responding.

If you find yourself in a place of being sold, told, or put on hold, there are times when you can rescue the conversation by floating out the proper buoy. Let's take a look at some potential conversation buoys you can attach to your discussion when experiencing conversational frustrations.

The Sold Buoy

If people are unwittingly selling, the conversation becomes a one-way discussion because they want you to feel their enthusiasm about their experiences and views. Let these individuals know that you appreciate their fervor and desire to help. Ask if they would be willing to entertain another idea or approach:

> "Thanks for telling me about your experience. I appreciate you sharing it. Could I get you to entertain an idea I'm playing around with at the moment?"

You are affirming these individuals and asking them to work with you. This approach fits the seller's psyche and is nonthreatening. If, on the other hand, you are dealing with more manipulative sellers, you need to be aware of the fact that they have no interest in your interests—their agenda is the only one that exists. Their goal is to transfer their intentions to you by dancing around your agenda. You could respond as follows:

> "You make a great point. In a lot of cases, I think it would work. I'm just not sure about this particular situation. Should I tell you more about it?"

You have subtly requested that they cease selling and simultaneously opened an opportunity to explain yourself. If the seller allows you to talk and hears what you have to say, you may rescue the conversation. If not, there was never going to be anything but a sales pitch anyway. Be aware that some willing sellers interpret "No" as "You need to sell me more" and will completely miss your invitation to hear you out and engage in dialogue.

The Told Buoy

When you're being told, you first need to understand that the teller is quite often driven by a *need to be right*. The difference between the unwitting and willful teller is that the former needs to be right as in *correct,* while the latter needs to be right as in *superior.* Being able to distinguish between the two is a matter of your ability to read tone and attitude.

Both unwitting and witting tellers come with a pre-conceived agenda and rocklike thinking, based on what *has* happened, not on what *is* happening or *could* happen. Tellers are often caught up with the past to the point that they cannot see the present or future. They can be master historians to the point that history colors or overrides the present and future possibilities. They are seeing one-third of the past, present, and future portrait because "facts are facts" and "what has happened" has been cemented into their thinking. You might say something like:

> "I agree that this has truly been the case in the past, but let's not allow that to overly influence what could be. It's possible we've learned some things from what has happened that we could apply here."

You are asking them to entertain the prospect of thinking outside of their own rationale. You are attempting to change the context from *you* to *us.*

The Put-On-Hold Buoy

Understand that put-on-hold people may not have cruel intentions but instead may lack a vision of what you want and revert to the status quo as a result. Unwitting delayers may be those individuals who struggle to decide or just are not convinced yet. You might steer the conversation by asking:

> "What do you think you would need to make a confident decision?" Or, "What next steps do you think you might be comfortable with in order to move forward?"

By doing this, you are addressing their reticence and ambivalence. You are affirming their need for caution and care in decision making. You are opening the door to baby steps and incremental progress, as opposed to irreversible decision and regret.

When confronting willful delayers—the chess masters who are looking for a path to put you in check or checkmate—realize that your possibilities are limited to their willingness to relinquish control. These are slim odds to start with. Your choices are limited to confronting their agenda with candor or playing chess master yourself and eventually forcing their hand. The latter is out of the bounds of conversation and in the realm of gamesmanship. If you choose the former (candor), you may want to try something like this:

"Can you tell me directly what you would like to see happen and why?"

You are indicating that you know their agenda is command and control and that they must have some good reason for wanting to stay in control. You are attempting to understand why they feel the need to move others toward or away from their goal. You may not open the door (of conversation) any further with this individual, but you won't know until you offer it. If they don't respond to your invitation, the reason is because they have already hung up—you just haven't heard the dial tone yet.

Now that we have explored and exposed the various forms of conversation counterfeit, we come to the final point of conversation. We will now offer the lynchpin for becoming a great conversationalist—making ourselves *accountable* in what others consider to be their most important conversations.

CHAPTER TEN

The Question That Sets You Apart

Conversation distinguishes the human being from the animal and the civilized man from the barbarian.
— *Michael Oakeshott, British Philosopher*

Mitch called Ron to express concerns about their business relationship. At that time, Mitch was a producer of educational videos and Ron's company was a leading distributor to schools in the United States. After a long discussion over breakfast regarding the future of their business relationship, Ron posed a very simple question to Mitch.

The question, spoken with integrity and sincerity, caused Mitch to sit back in his chair. He had never been asked this question before. It implied that Ron wanted

Mitch to gain what he deemed necessary from their conversation. While Mitch had always been impressed with Ron's manner, tone, and bearing, this was extraordinary to him—Ron was making himself accountable in a meeting that Mitch had requested. Ron's question was straightforward and perfectly timed: *"Have you received what you hoped for in our conversation today?"*

"Yes, Ron, as a matter of fact, I have. I'm very happy with the result of this conversation. Thank you for asking."

Ron not only heard Mitch but also listened. Ron responded with understanding and agreed to take steps to accommodate Mitch's requests. It became quite clear to Mitch how Ron had succeeded in building his company into an industry leader.

In the book, *Birth of the Chaordic Age,* Dee Hock tells the story of being a young banker and asking for a meeting with the president of his bank to discuss a serious concern he had about a project he was involved with.

The bank president answered his every request—beyond what Dee had hoped for. At the end of the conversation, he asked Dee, "Did the meeting serve your purpose?"

Dee responded with, "Yes. Yes. Thank you kindly."

The bank president then rose, shook his hand warmly, smiled, and said, "Thank you so much for coming to see me. Please let me know if I can be helpful at any time."[4]

Dee had asked for the meeting. It was his problem that was demanding attention, and the bank president was thanking *him* for the meeting. Dee Hock walked away from that meeting with a determination that he would never let that man down. He would never disappoint him for having helped him.

The project that Dee Hock was working on and needed help with was seminal and would become something we would all become familiar with—Dee Hock is the man who created the VISA card enterprise.

There was that question again: *"Did the meeting serve your purpose?"* While the wording was different from, *"Have you received what you hoped for in our conversation?"* the intent was the same—a sincere desire to help others improve their situation.

Dee Hock was deeply impressed by both the authenticity and tone of the question put to him by the bank president. He immediately adopted this conversational habit as his own business practice. *He made*

---

[4] Dee Hock, *Birth of the Chaordic Age* (San Francisco: Berrett-Koehler Publishers, 2000).

the decision to never let anyone walk away unfulfilled from a conversation with him. This quality of life decision would serve us all well—individually and collectively.

Dee Hock went on to do something extraordinary: he convinced thousands of banks to work cooperatively on lending credit—an unthinkable and highly improbable proposition in the 1960s. He credited his experience with the bank president as being a watershed moment in his life. He learned that in order to succeed, he needed to make sure he was genuinely helping others do the same. The perfect place for demonstrating this ethos was in conversation.

These stories are about two different business leaders who created two very distinct businesses, but they both have one simple but profound principle at work in their dealings with others—when they have a conversation with someone, they ensure that the other party leaves the conversation feeling a sense of progress and empowerment.

This is the spirit of the defining conversation.

So often we wonder if conversations are worth our time anymore. Defining conversations recognize the point of conversation that speaks to both the actual moment of conversation (it will never repeat itself in the same way again) and to its purpose (understanding and progress that will only be satisfied with mutuality and personal significance).

Defining conversations recognize the point of conversation which speaks to both the actual moment of conversation and to its purpose.

You can learn to be better prepared for important conversations by striving for greater awareness of what is at stake for others. This awareness begins with *recognizing* that

- **The other person has an expectation.**
- **If the expectation is not met, trust begins to tatter and the relationship begins to erode.**
- **There are specific emotional and factual points that you need to understand and progress toward.**

Begin imagining how your personal commitment to be accountable in conversation and to ask this question could change your course and improve your relationships. When you know you are going to ask "the question" at the end of your next important conversation, you instinctively make yourself accountable to deliver something of value both during and after the conversation. This commitment toward personal accountability leads to a heightened awareness in the course of conversation.

In this state of heightened awareness within conversation, you are now seeking to understand and empathize with the concern of the person you are talking to. All mental and emotional "hands" are on deck. You are focused. What do you need to know, and how will you discover that information in the time you have to converse? As you have already discovered, the answer is threefold: the point in time, your point of view, and the points of contact.

Point in Time

Point in time centers on the significance of the timing of this conversation—where you intuitively pick up on why the conversation is happening when it is happening. It is important to keep in mind that no moment ever repeats itself.

Point of View

Point of view centers on how the other person sees the situation and why. This is about validating someone as a human being and demonstrating that the conversation is about mutuality. Empathy is impossible until you hear someone else's views.

Points of Contact

Points of contact center on how the other party feels about the conversation and what he or she wants out of it. This is the point where both empathy and clarity are forged—where you discover the other person's concerns and goals, as well as the accompanying feelings. As a result, the other party gets the sense that progress will be made.

None of us can claim to be experts in conversation. We tend to behave differently as we move from conversation to conversation, depending on what we perceive to be at stake. But we can all lay claim to better intentions going forward. Hopefully, as a result of reading this book, you will have a greater grasp of what is at stake.

We all need to exercise discipline within our conversations that will lead to better interactions. If you desire to elevate your game as a leader, parent, spouse, or team player, you can do so with one simple discipline.

That discipline is to commit to asking some version of the question, *"Have you received what you hoped for in our conversation?"*

The question brings focus to all faculties necessary for success in conversation. You recognize that you are not in this conversation to "be heard loud and clear" or "to get your point across." This is the way others behave when communicating. This is especially true in conversations when others have come to you with what to them is a pressing concern. You need to hear their concern and respond with empathy and action. You need to hold yourself accountable.

By embracing accountability in conversation, you are motivated to form a framework for your inquiring— a framework that ensures you do not disappoint others. The framework of PIT (point in time), POV (point of view), and POC (points of contact) can help you understand each situation and person better. These mental touchstones will assist you in maintaining your awareness while engaged in conversation.

Becoming a great conversationalist is not just talking differently and listening more, but in being unique in how you think during those conversations.

We believe that a key to becoming a great conversationalist is not just talking differently and listening more, but also in being unique in how we *think* during those conversations. How we think can determine what we hear and miss, what we see and are blind to, what we perceive and what goes right over our head. There are important points to gather in every conversation (view, contact, timing)—if we miss one, we risk missing the entire point of the conversation. Thinking differently from others in the course of conversation differentiates us from all the rest.

Great conversationalists will not bring the conversation to a close until they are confident that they know

- **how the other person sees the matter;**
- **how the other person feels about the matter; and**
- **what it is that person really wants.**

The point of conversation is to walk away with answers to all three questions and for the other party to be cognizant that you have done so. "The question" is your way of saying, "I am making myself accountable in order to help you progress."

When is the last time you walked away from a conversation confident that all your important matters were addressed—your point of view was heard, your feelings on the matter were known, and a commitment to help you make progress was made? If you've ever had such an experience, you will understand what we mean by the term *conversated*. To be conversated means participating in a dialogue that leaves you satisfied.

In conversations, we have all observed that there are talkers and there are takers—but not a lot of conversaters. Dee Hock chose to be someone who made sure people walked away satisfied. His efforts changed the world as we know it. Great conversationalists want to be to be known and remembered in this way.

If you desire is to be a great conversationalist, begin looking for language that is comfortable for you, so that you can ask your own version of "the question" at the end of conversations when you sense that something of significance is at stake for the other party. You will do this because you sincerely want the other person to walk away filled with hope and confidence in you as a human being:

>"Have you received what you hoped for in our conversation?"
>
>"Has this meeting served your purpose?"
>
>"Has this conversation helped your situation?"

Find the words that fit your persona and express your spirit in a natural way as you reveal something quite extraordinary about yourself: *you are here to make a difference.*

We believe that if you commit yourself to asking this one profound question, your life will improve. We believe that by committing to ask this question, you are committing to follow through on your promises. Such noble behavior can only serve to increase your stature in all realms of influence.

We wish to leave you with this final thought: Be prepared for your next conversation because it could be defining in nature. And even if it is not, we are all ultimately defined by our conversations.

About the Authors

Scott West and Mitch Anthony have collaborated on three groundbreaking books on relationships in business. Their seminal work, *StorySelling for Financial Advisors* has been a perennial best seller for more than a decade, and was cited by *Financial Planning* magazine as the number one must-read book for the financial industry.

Scott West is Head of Consulting for Invesco VanKampen Consulting. He is a well-respected and popular speaker on a wide range of topics and is best known for his creative application of marketing strategies and concepts. Scott is coauthor of four books, including *StorySelling for Financial Advisors* and *The Language of Trust*.

scooterwest@sbcglobal.net

Mitch Anthony has been educating consumers and professionals about the importance of building lasting relationships and more meaningful lives for more than 20 years. His efforts in bringing transparency and responsibility to the financial services industry have earned him recognition as one of the industry's top "movers and shakers." Mitch is the author of 13 books, including *The New Retirementality* and *The Cash in the Hat*.

www.mitchanthony.com
mitch@mitchanthony.com

ISBN: 978-0-9727523-7-4